What Chefs Need to Know

W9-AWQ-620

Diane Lindsey Reeves

Published in the United States of America by Cherry Lake Publishing Group
Ann Arbor, Michigan
www.cherrylakepublishing.com

Reading Adviser: Beth Walker Gambro, MS, Ed., Reading Consultant, Yorkville, IL

Photo Credits: © Tonet Gandia/Shutterstock, cover, 1; © Semen Kuzmin/Shutterstock, 5; © ciazamfir/Shutterstock, 7; © Sterling Munksgard/Shutterstock, 8; Lynn Gilbert, CC BY-SA 4.0 via Wikimedia Commons, 9; © ekaterinaleto/Shutterstock, 11; © NP27/Shutterstock, 12; © Morenovel/Shutterstock, 13; © Alexander Raths/Shutterstock, 14; © anon_tae/Shutterstock, 17; © Kamil Macniak/Shutterstock, 18; © Africa Studio/Shutterstock, 19; © Komposit Studio/Shutterstock, 21; © U2M Brand/Shutterstock, 22; © Jacob Lund/Shutterstock, 23; © Suteren/Shutterstock, 24; © The Image Party/Shutterstock, 25; © Rawpixel.com/Shutterstock, 27; © PeopleImages.com - Yuri A/Shutterstock, 29

Copyright © 2024 by Cherry Lake Publishing Group

All rights reserved. No part of this book may be reproduced or utilized in any form or by any means without written permission from the publisher.

Cherry Lake Press is an imprint of Cherry Lake Publishing Group.

Library of Congress Cataloging-in-Publication Data

Names: Reeves, Diane Lindsey, 1959- author.
Title: What chefs need to know / written by Diane Lindsey Reeves.
Description: Ann Arbor, Michigan : Cherry Lake Publishing, [2024] | Series: Career expert files | Audience: Grades 4-6 | Summary: "Chefs need to have the expert knowledge, skills, and tools to feed the foodies of the world. The Career Expert Files series covers professionals who are experts in their fields. These career experts know things we never thought they'd need to know, but we're glad they do"— Provided by publisher.
Identifiers: LCCN 2023035041 | ISBN 9781668939116 (paperback) | ISBN 9781668938072 (hardcover) | ISBN 9781668940457 (ebook) | ISBN 9781668941805 (pdf)
Subjects: LCSH: Cooks—Juvenile literature. | Cooking—Vocational guidance—Juvenile literature.
Classification: LCC TX652.4 .R45 2024 | DDC 641.5—dc23/eng/20230911
LC record available at https://lccn.loc.gov/2023035041

Cherry Lake Publishing Group would like to acknowledge the work of the Partnership for 21st Century Learning, a Network of Battelle for Kids. Please visit Battelle for Kids online for more information.

Printed in the United States of America

Note from publisher: Websites change regularly, and their future contents are outside of our control. Supervise children when conducting any recommended online searches for extended learning opportunities.

Diane Lindsey Reeves likes to write books that help students figure out what they want to be when they grow up. She mostly lives in Washington, D.C., but spends as much time as she can in North Carolina and South Carolina with her grandkids.

CONTENTS

In the Know

Every career you can imagine has one thing in common. It takes an expert. Career experts need to know more about how to do a specific job than other people do. That's how everyone from plumbers to rocket scientists get their jobs done.

Sometimes it takes years of college study to learn what they need to know. Other times, people learn by working alongside someone who is already a career expert. No matter how they learn, it takes a career expert to do any job well.

Take chefs, for instance. The famous chefs you see on TV make their jobs look so glamorous and easy. The truth is, it took a lot of talent and skill to make it look that way.

Do you love good food and enjoy cooking? Would you like to **concoct** amazing dishes that make people say, "Wow"? Would you like to be a chef someday? Here are some things you need to know.

A Good Chef Is:

- Crazy about food
- Creative
- Not afraid of hard work
- A good leader
- Organized and able to multi-task

CHAPTER 1

Chefs Know...
All About Food

Foodies are people who are crazy about food. They like to eat it, of course. But they also like to cook it, read about it, and talk about it. They like trying new kinds of foods. Not every foodie is a chef. But it's safe to assume many chefs are foodies. Food is not only their job. It is their hobby and passion.

Foodies—and chefs—are especially interested in interesting food. They tend to be adventurous eaters. They're ready to try anything new. They are eager to try **cuisine** from different places.

Many foodies enjoy recording the new and interesting foods they eat!
Some post pictures of these foods to social media.

Chef Gordon Ramsay has been on many cooking television shows.

The best chefs are also very creative with food. They have a way of turning ordinary food into something amazing. They come up with new twists that make their dishes stand out.

Gordon Ramsay is a famous chef. He owns restaurants. He stars in TV shows about cooking. And he writes bestselling cookbooks. He is especially known for his Italian and French dishes.

Not many chefs achieve the celebrity status of Chef Ramsay. But they can learn a lot from chefs like him. He says that part of his success came from learning from other successful chefs. Aspiring chefs can follow his lead. Watching other chefs helps build skills and confidence. Working with other chefs can do the same! It can inspire future chefs and bring out their best foodie talents.

There is one thing that all good chefs do, famous or not. They create food that keeps people coming back for more.

FAMOUS FOODIES

Learn about other chefs who have made it big. Check out their cookbooks from the library. Julia Child, Guy Fieri, Rachel Ray, and Ina Garten have many fans. You can also do an online search for "famous chefs" to find plenty more.

CHAPTER 2

Chefs Know...
How to Cook Great Food

There's so much more to cooking than popping food into a microwave. Chefs must know how to prepare food in many ways. Certain foods taste better when cooked in certain ways. Good chefs know which cooking method to use with which foods.

Here are common ways to cook food:

- Baking involves placing foods inside a preheated oven. In the oven, they are cooked in a dry heat. Bread, cakes, cookies, and other baked goods are made this way.

Baking foods is a slow drying-out process of whatever is in the oven.

- Blanching involves briefly cooking food in **boiling** water. Then you instantly stop the cooking process by dipping the food in icy cold water. Blanching brings out the best flavors in fresh vegetables. It also makes it easier to peel fruits like tomatoes and peaches.

- Boiling is a way to cook pasta and other dishes. This involves cooking food in a pot of boiling water. Cook it to the desired doneness.

- Braising uses wet and dry heat. Braising is used to cook meats and root vegetables. First, the food is browned at a high temperature. Then it is simmered in liquid, such as gravy, inside a covered pot. Stews and pot roasts are delicious when prepared this way.

A GOOD EGG

Eggs are nutritious and can be delicious. They are also easy to cook on a stove. You can boil, fry, or poach them. You can also scramble them. Or you can get extra fancy. Add chopped meat and vegetables to create an **omelet**. What is your favorite way to eat eggs?

Different pastas require different boiling times—make sure to check the package or the recipe!

Many people grill outside, especially in the summer. Chefs also use this method in the kitchen.

- Broiling is a quick cooking method for tender meat. It's also used for poultry or fish. Broiling is done in the oven at a high temperature. The heat comes from above the food.

- Deep frying is when food is submerged in hot oil. It is cooked to a brown, crispy finish. Hello, french fries!

- Grilling is a quick cooking method. Food is cooked on a rack using a grill. The grill can be gas, electric, charcoal, or wood. This method is popular for summer cookouts.

- Pan-frying involves frying food in a skillet on a stove. Cooking oil or fat helps keep the food from sticking to the pan.

- Poaching is a gentle way to cook foods like fish and eggs. Food is submerged in a liquid. It is cooked at a low temperature. This temperature is just below the boiling point.

- Roasting uses the dry heat of an oven. This dry heat surrounds food with hot air. This process cooks food evenly on all sides. Thanksgiving turkeys are often cooked this way.

- Sautéing is when food is cooked quickly over high heat. It is cooked in a small amount of oil. Sometimes no oil is used. Some recipes call for onions or mushrooms to be sautéed. This method is also used to make gravy. Gravy or other sauces are made from juices left in the pan.

- Steaming involves a smaller pot or steamer filled with food. This is placed over a pot of boiling water. Cover the outer pot to create steam. This is a way to prepare broccoli and asparagus.

CHAPTER 3

Chefs Know... How to Find Their Way Around a Kitchen

Commercial kitchens come in all shapes and sizes. They serve lots of food to lots of people. That's why you'll find tools in commercial kitchens that you won't find at home.

The first tool even home cooks need is a good set of knives. So much food preparation involves cutting, chopping, and slicing. Chefs keep their knives sharp. They bring their own knives with them. They store their knives in a leather **knife roll**.

A favorite knife is the 8– to 10–inch (20.3 to 25.4 centimeters) chef's knife. Chefs use this all-purpose knife often. Utility, paring, and bread knives are also in their knife rolls. Chefs also use boning knives and cleavers.

Chefs practice knife safety by keeping their knives very sharp. Dull knives need more force to cut, and so can slip more easily and cut the chef instead of the food.

Chefs need to keep their stations (and kitchens) very clean. This makes food safe to eat and cuts down on kitchen accidents.

Chefs use many of the same tools as home cooks. They use pots, pans, bowls, and measuring cups. The main difference is that their tools are bigger. They also use more of them.

Restaurant kitchens need different types of cooking equipment. They have ovens, stoves, grills, and deep fryers.

Commercial kitchens also need equipment to keep food cold. They use refrigerators and freezers like you use at home. But theirs store more food.

They have walk-in cooler rooms. Food can be organized and easily reached in these rooms. Many restaurants also have ice machines and beverage dispensers.

You'll also find preparation, or prep, tools in a chef's kitchen. They include commercial mixers used to make bread and pizza dough. A home mixer can hold 5 to 7 quarts (4.7 to 6.6 liters) of ingredients. The biggest commercial mixers can hold up to 200 quarts (189.3 L)!

Sturdy prep tables are used at each kitchen station. Other prep tools include blenders and food processors.

A well-run commercial kitchen is organized and clean. Every tool has a place. Chefs count on being able to find the right tool when they need it.

DREAM KITCHEN

Ask an adult to help you go online. Search for images and descriptions of tools used by chefs. Print out images and make labels for each tool you find. Make a collage showing a chef's dream kitchen.

CHAPTER 4

Chefs Know...
How to Cook Safely

Chefs know that there are many ways to get hurt in a kitchen. They quickly learn how to avoid common hazards. Some lessons are learned the hard way. Others come by training.

Burns and cuts are obvious **occupational hazards** for chefs. Accidents happen when working with heat and sharp knives.

That's one reason why learning knife skills is so important. You cannot become a chef without them. Chefs learn how to properly grip a knife. They also learn to tuck the fingers of their helping hand into a bear claw to avoid chopping them off. These skills result in professionally prepared food. They also result in fewer cuts and injuries.

Going slow to perfect safe knife skills first helps chefs a lot in the long run.

Kitchen fires can start quickly and spread quickly. Chefs need to pay attention while they're cooking.

It's easy to get burned in a kitchen. The most common way is from leaving food unattended. This can cause food to boil over. It can also cause a kitchen fire. Chefs teach themselves not to do it.

Chefs also learn to stay in their lanes to stay safe. This is why special stations are set up for each type of food preparation. Injuries are prevented when chefs work where they belong.

Keeping a kitchen clean prevents slips on spilled food. Keeping it organized prevents staff from tripping over misplaced supplies.

TRUE OR FALSE

The proper way to wash your hands is to scrub them with soap and water for as long as it takes to sing the "Happy Birthday" song twice.

Silly, but true. It takes washing with soap for at least 20 seconds to remove germs from your hand. Don't forget your fingertips and thumbs!

Certain foods are considered cooked at specific temperatures. This ensures all bacteria is killed off and the food is safe to eat.

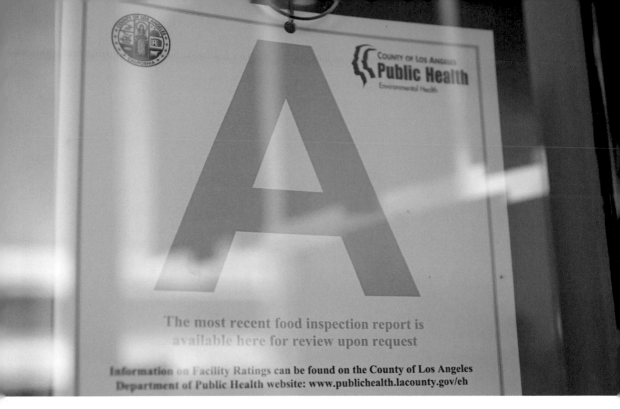

Health inspections regularly occur at restaurants. An "A" is the highest rating.

Foodborne illness is another serious kitchen hazard. Chefs must be extremely careful to use fresh, clean ingredients. Ingredients that have gone bad can make customers sick. It can also damage a chef's **reputation**.

A chef's first priority is safety. They work to keep themselves, their staff, and their customers safe. When that happens, everything else is icing on the cake.

CHAPTER 5

Chefs Know...How to Find the Job They Want

There's no such thing as too many cooks in the kitchen when it comes to fine dining. It takes chefs with special skills to create food magic. They work together to create everything from main **entrées** to desserts.

The most common types of chefs:

- The executive or head chef is the top chef in a kitchen. They manage the kitchen, create new recipes, and plan the menus. Sometimes they own their own restaurants.

- *Sous chef* means "under chief" in French. A sous chef works directly with the head chef. They also help supervise other chefs. They plan schedules and train staff. They also prepare food and can assist at any of the kitchen stations.

Each chef in a kitchen has a specific job—that's how they keep things running smoothly and efficiently.

- Sauce chefs, or sauciers, are third in the lineup of chefs. They prepare salad dressing, pasta sauce, gravy, stews, stocks, and soups.

- Senior chefs oversee one station in a kitchen. They're responsible for making sure that only the best quality food leaves the station.

- Pastry chefs are responsible for making the bread, desserts, and pastries. They may also plan the dessert menu. Sometimes they create new desserts.

- Pantry chefs prepare dishes like salads and other cold foods. They also prepare cold items needed by other chefs. They tend to work in larger restaurants.

- Butcher chefs prepare the right types and cuts of meat needed in each workstation. Some kitchens also have fry chefs, grill chefs, and fish chefs.

COOK VERSUS CHEF

Chefs have more responsibilities in a kitchen than cooks. They often plan menus, manage budgets, and handle food orders. They may also manage other chefs and cooks. Cooks make food. That's what they do.

Some chefs come up with a new menu every day based on what fresh food is available.

- Prep chefs get an earlier start than other chefs. Their job is to prepare ingredients needed for different dishes. They may help with baking bread, cutting vegetables, and making foods that can be stored until needed.

- Commis chefs, or junior chefs, are entry-level chefs. They are just learning how to work in a kitchen. They help other chefs and keep work areas clean. They also gather ingredients and tools needed in different stations.

Teamwork helps chefs come together like the flavors of a delicious dish!

Activity

Stop, Think, and Write

Can you imagine a world without chefs? What if everyone always had to cook their own food?

Get a separate sheet of paper. On one side, answer these questions:

- *How do chefs make the world a better place?*
- *What do you think it would be like to work in a fancy restaurant or bake amazing desserts for weddings and other big events?*
- *Imagine you ran the best restaurant in town. What kind of food would it serve? What kinds of chefs would work there?*

On the other side of the paper:

- *Draw a picture of you preparing a gourmet meal fit for a king or celebrity!*

Things to Do If You Want to Be a Chef

Preparing to be a chef starts now, no matter how old you are. All you need is a kitchen, a favorite recipe, fresh ingredients, and adult supervision. From there, it takes training, experience, and luck. **Bon appétit**!

NOW

- Ask a trusted adult to show you how to make their favorite dishes.
- Look for cookbooks for kids at your local and school libraries and try out some new recipes.
- Watch cooking shows and competitions on TV.
- Take a cooking class for kids at a community center.
- Talk to a chef or baker about their job.

LATER

- Sign up for cooking classes in middle school and high school.
- Get a job in a restaurant to see what it's like to work in a kitchen.
- Enroll in a **culinary** arts program at a community college or technical school.
- Consider getting a 4-year college degree in culinary arts.

Learn More

Books

America's Test Kitchen. *Kids Can Cook Anything.* Boston, MA: America's Test Kitchen, 2022.

American Test Kitchen. *The Complete Cookbook for Young Chefs.* Naperville, IL: Sourcebooks Explore, 2018.

D'Amico, Joan, and Karen E. Drummond. *The Science Chef: 100 Fun Food Experiments and Recipes for Kids.* Hoboken, NJ: Jossey-Bass, 2020.

Master Chef Junior. *Master Chef Junior Cookbook.* New York, NY: Clarkson Potter, 2017.

On the Web

With an adult, learn more online with these suggested searches.

Cooking for Kids

Famous Chefs

Food Network Cooking Shows

USDA for Kids

Glossary

boiling (BOY-ling) cooking a liquid such as water until it reaches a temperature of 212°F (100°C) and is bubbling and steaming

bon appétit (BOHN ah-pay-TEE) a French phrase that means "enjoy your meal"

commercial kitchens (kuh-MUHR-shuhl KIH-chuhnz) kitchens designed for business use where food is sold to customers

concoct (kuhn-KAHKT) to make something by combing several different ingredients

cuisine (kwih-ZEEN) a style of cooking that involves special ingredients and dishes known to be common to a specific culture or country

culinary (KUH-luh-nair-ee) of or about the kitchen or cooking

entrées (AHN-trayz) dishes that make up the main course of a meal

knife roll (NIYF ROHL) a leather knife bag chefs use to store and safely transport their knives

occupational hazard (ah-kyuh-PAY-shuh-nuhl HA-zuhrd) risk that comes from working a specific type of job

omelet (AHM-luht) a dish of beaten eggs cooked in a frying pan until firm, often filled with cheese, vegetables, and meat and folded over before serving

reputation (re-pyuh-TAY-shuhn) the way other people view your worth or character

Index